HOW TO BE A SUCCESS AT ANYTHING

"Unlock the secrets to success with The little book of success, Discover the mindset, strategies and tactics used by the world's most successful individuals and learn how to apply them to your own life. Achieve your goals, build your dreams and live the life you've always wanted with the practical and powerful guidance in the little book of success and How to become a success at anything!

To become successful in anything, it is important to set specific, measurable, and achievable goals. Create a plan and take consistent, focused action towards achieving those goals. Continuously evaluate and adjust your plan as needed. Seek out resources, mentorship, and opportunities to learn and grow. Stay persistent and don't give up, even when faced with obstacles. It is also important to maintain a positive mindset and believe in yourself.

Money can certainly be a useful tool for achieving success, but it is not the only factor, and it is not always necessary to have a significant amount of money in order to be successful. Many successful people have started with very little and worked hard to achieve their goals. The key is to have a clear plan and take consistent, focused action towards achieving your goals, regardless of the amount of money you have available. Of course, having more money can provide more resources and opportunities, but it is important to remember that money is not the only determining factor for success.

There are many factors that can contribute to becoming successful, but some of the major determining factors include:

Setting clear, specific and achievable goals: Having a clear vision of what you want to achieve and a plan for how to get there is essential for success.

Taking consistent, focused action: Successful people take consistent, focused action towards achieving their goals. They do not let distractions or setbacks deter them from their purpose.

Willingness to learn and grow: Successful people are always learning and growing, they are open to new ideas and are willing to take risks.

Staying resilient and persistent: Successful people don't give up easily, they stay resilient and persistent in the face of obstacles and challenges.

Strong work ethic: Successful people tend to have a strong work ethic, they are disciplined and dedicated in their pursuits.

Networking and building relationships: Successful people know how to build and maintain strong relationships, they understand the importance of networking and building a strong support system.

Self-discipline and self-motivation: Successful people have the ability to stay motivated and disciplined, they are able to focus on their goals and take action even when they don't feel like it.

Having a growth mindset: Successful people have a growth mindset, they understand that failure is a natural part of the learning process and they use it to improve themselves.

It's worth noting that success can also be subjective, what may be considered a success for one person may not be for another, and the factors that lead to success in one field or area may not be the same as those in another field.

The most lucrative fields can vary depending on the current market conditions and can change over time. Some fields that have traditionally been considered lucrative include finance, technology, healthcare, and real estate. However, it is important to note that earning a high salary does not necessarily equate to success.

In the technology industry, fields such as artificial intelligence, big data, and cloud computing are in high demand and have the potential to be lucrative. In the healthcare industry, positions in fields such as biotechnology, pharmaceuticals, and medical devices can be financially rewarding.

In the finance industry, positions in investment banking, private equity, and hedge funds can be lucrative. In the real estate industry, positions such as real estate developer, commercial broker and property manager can be financially rewarding.

It's also important to consider what is important to you in your career, what you're passionate about and what aligns with your values, as those factors will lead to a more fulfilling and satisfying career. Success is not only measured by financial gain, but also by personal fulfillment and satisfaction in your chosen field. It's important to find a balance between choosing a field with potential for financial success and one that aligns with your interests and values.

It is difficult to pinpoint a specific field of business that has the most potential for financial success, as it can vary depending on the current market conditions and can change over time. However, some business fields that have traditionally been considered to have high potential for financial success include:

Technology: The technology industry is constantly evolving and fields such as artificial intelligence, big data, and cloud computing are in high demand and have the potential to be lucrative.

Healthcare: The healthcare industry is also a rapidly growing field, with positions in fields such as biotechnology, pharmaceuticals, and medical devices offering the potential for financial success.

Finance: The finance industry, specifically investment banking, private equity, and hedge funds, also tend to offer high earning potential.

Real Estate: Real estate development and investment can be a profitable business, especially if you have the knowledge, skills, and capital to navigate the market.

E-commerce and Online Business: With the rise of internet and mobile usage, the e-commerce and online business fields have high potential for financial success as well.

It's worth noting that success in these fields also depend on an individual's skills, knowledge, experience and ability to adapt to changing market conditions. It's important to conduct your own research and due diligence when considering a career in any field.

When conducting research to achieve success in any field, some methods that may be useful include:

Networking: Talk to people who are currently working in the field you are interested in and ask for their advice and insights. Attend industry events and conferences to meet and connect with professionals in your desired field.

Reading: Research the industry and read articles, books, and reports on trends and best practices. Stay up-to-date on the latest developments in your field by subscribing to relevant publications and newsletters.

Online Research: Utilize online resources such as industry specific websites, forums, and social media groups to learn more about the field and the current trends.

Job Shadowing: Job shadowing is a great way to gain hands-on experience and learn about the day-to-day operations of a particular job or industry.

Internship: If possible, look for internships or apprenticeships in your desired field. This will give you the opportunity to learn from experienced professionals and gain real-world experience.

Get a mentor: Having a mentor who is experienced and successful in your desired field can be very valuable. They can give you guidance, advice and can help you avoid common mistakes.

It's important to keep in mind that the research process is an ongoing process and it's important to stay informed and adapt to the changes in the field. Additionally, it is important to use various sources and not rely on a single source as research can be biased.

Success and happiness are two different things, and it is possible to have one without the other. Success is often defined as achieving a specific goal or accomplishment, such as a promotion, a successful business, or a high salary. On the other hand, happiness is a subjective feeling of well-being and contentment.

While achieving success can bring a sense of accomplishment and satisfaction, it is not a guarantee of happiness. Many successful people have reported feeling unfulfilled or unhappy despite their achievements. Happiness is more likely to come from a sense of purpose, a positive outlook on life, and healthy relationships with others.

It is important to find a balance between striving for success and striving for happiness. Success can bring happiness, but it is not the only thing that can bring happiness. It's important to also focus on building meaningful relationships, practicing self-care and developing a sense of purpose. One may also find happiness in helping others, volunteering and/or contributing to a cause that aligns with their values. In short, happiness comes from a combination of things and success is just one of them.

Happiness is a subjective feeling of well-being and contentment. It is a complex emotion that can be influenced by a variety of factors such as genetics, environment, and personal circumstances.

There are several ways one can achieve happiness, here are a few:

Cultivate Positive Relationships: Strong relationships with family and friends can provide a sense of belonging and support, which can lead to increased happiness.

Practice gratitude: Being grateful for what you have can help shift your focus from what you lack to what you have, and increase your overall satisfaction and happiness.

Find purpose and meaning: Having a sense of purpose in life, such as a meaningful career, a passion, or a cause to contribute to, can give life a sense of meaning and fulfillment.

Engage in self-care: Taking care of your physical, emotional and mental well-being can promote happiness and reduce stress.

Practice mindfulness and meditation: Mindfulness practices such as meditation can help you become more present, reduce stress and increase feelings of calm and well-being.

Engage in activities that bring you joy: Engaging in activities that you enjoy, whether it's a hobby, sport, or creative pursuit, can bring a sense of fulfillment and happiness.

It's important to note that happiness is a fluid state, and it can change from day to day, person to person. What may make one person happy may not work for the other person. It's important to find what works for you and make it a consistent practice in your life.

Work-life balance refers to the balance between an individual's professional and personal responsibilities, and the ability to manage them in a way that allows for a healthy, fulfilling lifestyle. It can be defined as the equilibrium between time and energy devoted to work and time and energy devoted to personal and family life.

There are several ways to achieve a better work-life balance

Set boundaries: Clearly define the hours you will work and when you will not be available, and communicate these boundaries to your colleagues and supervisor.

Prioritize: Prioritize your tasks and focus on the most important ones first. This will help you manage your time more efficiently.

Learn to say no: Saying no to unnecessary obligations and commitments can help you focus on what's important and avoid overloading your schedule.

Take breaks: Taking regular breaks throughout the day can help you recharge and improve productivity.

Make time for yourself: Make time for hobbies, exercise, relaxation, and other activities that bring you joy and fulfillment.

Communicate with your employer: Talk to your employer about your work-life balance needs and see if there are ways to work together to create a more balanced schedule.

Work-life balance is different for everyone and it's important to find a balance that works for you. It's important to review your schedule and responsibilities regularly and make adjustments as needed. Remember that it's important to make time for yourself and your loved ones, in order to have a fulfilling life.

Set specific and achievable goals: Having clear and specific goals can help you stay focused and motivated.

Prioritize tasks: Prioritize your tasks based on importance and urgency, and tackle the most important ones first.

Create a schedule: Plan your day in advance and schedule your time in blocks to increase productivity.

Eliminate distractions: Identify and eliminate any distractions that may be preventing you from staying focused on your work.

Take breaks: Taking short breaks regularly can help prevent burnout and increase productivity.

Use a timer: Use a timer to track the amount of time you spend on each task, this can help you stay on task and avoid procrastination.

Delegate tasks: Delegate tasks to others if possible, this can free up your time to focus on more important tasks.

Use tools and technology: Utilize tools and technology such as apps, software and other productivity tools to manage your time and boost productivity

Stay organized: Keep your workspace and digital files organized to help you stay on top of your tasks and reduce stress.

Take care of your physical and mental well-being: Taking care of your physical and mental well-being by getting enough sleep, eating well, and exercising can help improve your productivity levels.

It's worth noting that what works for one person may not work for another, it's important to find what works best for you and adapt accordingly. And also to be consistent with the habits you choose to implement in order to see the best results.

Create a budget: Start by creating a budget and tracking your spending to understand your income and expenses.

Reduce expenses: Look for ways to reduce your expenses, such as cutting back on subscriptions and memberships, eating out less, and shopping for deals.

Increase income: Look for ways to increase your income, such as taking on a side hustle, asking for a raise, or starting a business.

Invest: Invest your money in assets that have the potential to appreciate in value, such as stocks, real estate, or a small business.

Save: Make saving money a priority, set a goal and create a plan to reach it.

Pay off debt: Pay off high-interest debt as quickly as possible to reduce the amount of interest you pay over time.

Create multiple streams of income: Diversify your income streams by investing in different assets, such as stocks, bonds, or rental properties.

Live below your means: Spend less than you earn, and avoid lifestyle inflation.

Educate yourself: Learn about personal finance, investing, and money management so you can make informed decisions.

Seek professional advice: Consider working with a financial advisor or planner to help you create a plan and stay on track with your financial goals.

It's worth noting that becoming financially free takes time, discipline and persistence. It's important to start early and make it a habit, and to review your progress regularly to make adjustments as needed.

Self-sabotage refers to the act of intentionally or unintentionally undermining one's own success. Here are a few ways people may self-sabotage their own success:

Procrastination: Putting things off or delaying taking action towards a goal can prevent success from being achieved.

Perfectionism: Holding oneself to unrealistic standards and being unable to move forward if things are not perfect can hinder progress and success.

Fear of failure: Fearing failure can prevent individuals from taking risks and trying new things, which can limit their potential for success.

Negative self-talk: Believing that one is not capable, worthy or deserving of success can prevent individuals from achieving their goals.

Self-doubt: Second guessing oneself and constantly questioning one's abilities can prevent individuals from taking action towards their goals.

Lack of focus: Being easily distracted, multitasking, and trying to do too many things at once can prevent individuals from making progress towards their goals.

Lack of persistence: Giving up too easily, not learning from mistakes and not being resilient in the face of challenges can prevent individuals from achieving success.

Not setting goals: Not having a clear idea of what one wants to achieve and not setting specific, measurable and achievable goals can limit one's potential for success.

Not seeking help: Not asking for help or not seeking guidance from others, such as mentors or experts, can prevent individuals from achieving their goals.

Not learning from failure: Not learning from failure and not taking responsibility for mistakes can prevent individuals from growing and achieving success.

It's important to recognize these behaviors and work on overcoming them in order to achieve success.

There are several reasons why people may sabotage their own success:

Fear of failure: Many people have a fear of failure, which can prevent them from taking risks and trying new things. They may sabotage their own success to avoid the possibility of failure.

Fear of success: Some people may have a fear of success, they may be afraid of the responsibilities and changes that come with success, and may sabotage their own success to avoid it.

Lack of self-esteem: People with low self-esteem may not believe they are capable of achieving success, and may sabotage their own efforts to avoid proving themselves wrong.

Unresolved past traumas: People who have unresolved past traumas may sabotage their own success as a self-protective mechanism, as they may not be ready to face the challenges that come with success.

Comfort zone: People who are comfortable with their current situation may sabotage their own success as the thought of change and stepping out of their comfort zone can be scary and overwhelming.

Self-sabotage as a defense mechanism: Some people use self-sabotage as a defense mechanism, it can be a way to protect themselves from the disappointment and pain of failure.

Lack of a support system: People who lack a support system, or who have a negative support system, may sabotage their own success,

What are the signs of self sabotage and how to overcome them

Here are some signs that you may be self-sabotaging and ways to overcome them:

Procrastination: If you find yourself consistently putting things off or delaying taking action towards your goals, it may be a sign of self-sabotage. To overcome this, try breaking down tasks into smaller chunks, set specific deadlines, and hold yourself accountable.

Perfectionism: Holding yourself to unrealistic standards and being unable to move forward if things are not perfect can be a sign of self-sabotage. To overcome this, try to focus on progress rather than perfection and give yourself permission to make mistakes.

Fear of failure: If you find yourself avoiding taking risks or trying new things due to a fear of failure, it may be a sign of self-sabotage. To overcome this, try reframing your thoughts, practice visualization and focus on the benefits of taking risks.

Negative self-talk: Believing that you are not capable, worthy or deserving of success can be a sign of self-sabotage. To overcome this, try practicing positive self-talk, focus on your strengths and accomplishments, and challenge negative thoughts.

Self-doubt: Second-guessing yourself and constantly questioning your abilities can be a sign of self-sabotage. To overcome this, try building confidence through taking on small challenges, focus on your successes, and surround yourself with positive people.

Lack of focus: Being easily distracted, multitasking, and trying to do too many things at once can be a sign of self-sabotage. To overcome this, try setting specific goals, creating a schedule, and eliminating distractions.

Lack of persistence: Giving up too easily, not learning from mistakes and not being resilient in the face of challenges can be a sign of self-sabotage. To overcome this, try staying focus on your goals, learning from failure, and develop a growth mindset.

Not setting goals: Not having a clear idea of what you want to achieve and not setting specific, measurable and achievable goals

Self-belief, also known as self-confidence, is an important factor in becoming successful. It is the belief in one's own abilities, qualities, and judgments. Self-belief can influence a person's thoughts, emotions, and actions, and plays a significant role in achieving success.

Having self-belief can help individuals take action towards their goals, persevere through challenges, and make decisions that align with their values and aspirations. It allows individuals to trust their own abilities and to believe in their capacity to achieve success. People with self-belief tend to have a positive outlook on life, they are resilient, they tend to learn from their mistakes, they are less likely to procrastinate and are more likely to take action.

On the other hand, a lack of self-belief can lead to self-doubt, fear of failure, and a lack of motivation, which can prevent individuals from taking action towards their goals and limit their potential for success.

It's important to note that self-belief can be developed and strengthened over time through setting and achieving goals, learning from failures, and building a support system. Surrounding oneself with positive and supportive people, practicing self-care and self-compassion, and learning from mistakes can all help to build self-belief. Additionally, setting realistic and achievable goals, and celebrating progress and small wins can help to build self-belief, and increase the likelihood of achieving success.

Enemies of self belief

There are several factors that can act as enemies to self-belief, here are a few:

Negative self-talk: Repeated negative thoughts about oneself, such as "I'm not good enough" or "I can't do this" can erode self-belief.

Fear of failure: A fear of failure can lead to self-doubt and prevent individuals from taking action towards their goals.

Lack of self-awareness: A lack of self-awareness can prevent individuals from understanding their own strengths and weaknesses, and can lead to self-doubt.

Unresolved past traumas: Unresolved past traumas can affect an individual's self-worth and self-esteem, and can lead to self-doubt and lack of self-belief.

Social comparison: Comparing oneself to others and feeling inferior can lead to low self-esteem and self-doubt.

Perfectionism: Holding oneself to unrealistic standards can lead to feelings of inadequacy and self-doubt.

Lack of support: Not having a supportive environment or a lack of positive role models can lead to self-doubt and lack of self-belief.

Comparison with others: Seeing others achieve their goals, or comparing oneself to others who seem to have it all together can lead to self-doubt, and erode self-belief.

It's important to recognize these enemies of self-belief and to work on overcoming them. Building self-awareness, challenging negative thoughts, setting realistic goals, surrounding oneself with positive and supportive people, and seeking professional help can all be effective ways to overcome these enemies of self-belief and increase self-confidence.

Does self belief always equal success

Self-belief, also known as self-confidence, is an important factor in achieving success, but it is not the only factor. Self-belief is the belief in one's own abilities, qualities, and judgments, and it can help individuals take action towards their goals, persevere through challenges, and make decisions that align with their values and aspirations. However, self-belief alone does not guarantee success.

Success is a complex and multi-faceted concept that can be influenced by a variety of factors such as skills, knowledge, resources, and circumstances. Success also means different things to different people, and it can be achieved in different ways.

Self-belief is important because it can help individuals to overcome obstacles and challenges, and to take the necessary steps to achieve their goals. However, it's important to note that self-belief needs to be combined with other factors such as hard work, persistence, learning from failure and taking action.

It's also important to note that self-belief is not a constant state, it can fluctuate depending on the situation and an individual's personal circumstances. It's important to work on building and maintaining self-belief, but also to be aware that it's not the only factor that leads to success.

Self-belief and arrogance are two different things, although they may appear similar on the surface.

Self-belief is the belief in one's own abilities, qualities, and judgments. It is a healthy and positive form of self-confidence that helps individuals take action towards their goals, persevere through challenges, and make decisions that align with their values and aspirations.

Arrogance, on the other hand, is an excessive sense of self-importance. It is characterized by an inflated view of oneself and a belief that one is superior to others. Arrogant individuals often overestimate their abilities and believe that they are entitled to special privileges or treatment. They tend to be dismissive of others and may have difficulty accepting constructive criticism or feedback.

Arrogance can be detrimental to achieving success as it can lead to poor decision making, lack of accountability, and a lack of empathy towards others. It can also create negative impressions on others, which can affect a person's personal and professional relationships.

Self-belief is important for achieving success, but it should not be confused with arrogance. It's important to have a healthy level of self-confidence without crossing the line into arrogance. It's important to acknowledge and appreciate your own strengths and abilities but also to have humility, and be open to feedback and learning from others.

Warning Signs that you are becoming arrogant

Here are a few warning signs that you may be becoming arrogant:

You have a tendency to belittle or dismiss others opinions and ideas.

You believe that you are always right and that others are wrong.

You have a hard time accepting constructive criticism or feedback.

You have a tendency to boast or brag about your accomplishments.

You have a sense of entitlement and believe that you deserve special privileges or treatment.

You have a tendency to interrupt or talk over others in conversations.

You have a tendency to disregard the feelings and needs of others.

You have a tendency to blame others for your mistakes or shortcomings.

You have a tendency to disregard rules and regulations that do not suit you.

You have a tendency to be dismissive of others who are not like you or do not share your beliefs.

It's important to recognize these warning signs and take steps to address them. Arrogance can be detrimental to achieving success as it can lead to poor decision making, lack of accountability, and a lack of empathy towards others. It can also create negative impressions on others, which can affect a person's personal and professional relationships.

It's important to work on building humility and empathy, being open to feedback and learning from others, and to practice active listening and try to understand other perspectives.

Arrogance can undermine success in several ways:

Poor decision-making: Arrogant individuals often believe that they are always right, and may ignore advice or input from others, leading to poor decision-making.

Lack of accountability: Arrogant individuals may believe that they are above mistakes and may not take responsibility for their actions, leading to a lack of accountability.

Difficulty accepting constructive criticism: Arrogant individuals may have a hard time accepting constructive criticism or feedback, which can prevent them from learning and improving.

Lack of empathy: Arrogant individuals may have a lack of empathy and disregard the feelings and needs of others, which can lead to a lack of trust and cooperation from others.

Alienating others: Arrogant individuals may have a tendency to belittle or dismiss others, which can lead to alienation and a lack of support from others.

Poor communication: Arrogant individuals may have a tendency to interrupt or talk over others in conversations, which can lead to poor communication and a lack of understanding from others.

Stagnation: Arrogance may lead to a lack of learning and personal growth, preventing individuals from developing new skills and knowledge which can lead to stagnation in their careers.

Damaged reputation: Arrogance may lead to negative impressions on others, which can damage an individual's reputation, both professionally and personally.

It's important to recognize the ways in which arrogance can undermine success and to take steps to address it. Building humility and empathy, being open to feedback and learning from others, and practicing active listening can help to mitigate the negative effects of arrogance.

Successful people often have certain habits, traits, and strategies that they keep to themselves, which contribute to their success.

Here are a few examples of secrets that successful people may keep to themselves:

They have a clear vision and goal: Successful people often have a clear vision of what they want to achieve and a plan for how to get there. They are able to focus on their goals and stay motivated, even when faced with obstacles.

They take calculated risks: Successful people understand that taking risks is a necessary part of achieving success, but they also know when to take calculated risks and when to avoid unnecessary risks.

They are resilient: Successful people know that setbacks and failures are a natural part of the journey to success. They have the ability to bounce back from failure and continue moving forward.

They stay organized: Successful people often have a system for staying organized, whether it be a physical planner, a digital calendar, or a specific method for prioritizing tasks.

They are lifelong learners: Successful people understand that learning is a lifelong process, and they make a point to continue learning and growing, both personally and professionally.

They surround themselves with successful people: Successful people understand the power of networking and they surround themselves with people who are successful and can offer guidance and support.

They practice self-discipline and self-control: Successful people have the ability to control their impulses and emotions, they have the discipline to delay gratification and stay focused on their goals.

They have a positive attitude: Successful people often have a positive attitude, they look for the good in every situation, they have a growth mindset and are able to see challenges as opportunities for growth and learning.

They are adaptable: Successful people are able to adapt to change, they are flexible and can pivot when necessary. They are not afraid of change, they embrace it and find ways to make it work for them.

They are consistent: Successful people are consistent in their actions and in the pursuit of their goals. They don't give up easily and they are persistent in the face of obstacles.

They have a good work-life balance: Successful people understand the importance of taking care of themselves, they make time for themselves, their family and their hobbies, they don't let work consume all of their time.

They practice self-care: Successful people understand the importance of taking care of their physical, emotional and mental well-being. They make self-care a priority and prioritize activities that nourish their mind and body.

It's important to note that everyone's success journey is different, and what works for one person may not work for another. However, these are some common habits, traits, and strategies that successful people tend to keep to themselves and apply in their lives.

Will people love me if become successful

Success does not guarantee that people will love you, as love and success are separate concepts. Success can bring admiration and respect from others, but it does not necessarily mean that people will love you.

Love is a complex and multi-faceted emotion that is based on a variety of factors such as shared values, mutual respect, and understanding. Success can be one of the many factors that can contribute to a positive relationship, but it is not the only factor.

Additionally, some people may be envious of your success and may not show love or support. In other cases, you may find that your success changes the dynamics of your relationships and may cause some people to distance themselves from you.

It's important to remember that people will love you for who you are, not for your success. Having a strong sense of self-worth and building healthy relationships based on mutual respect, trust and understanding are key for a fulfilling life.

It's important to prioritize meaningful connections, communication and understanding with the people you care about, and to surround yourself with people who love and support you. It's also important to be open to feedback and to listen to others' perspectives, as it can help you to understand and strengthen your relationships

Is money the root of all evil

The phrase "money is the root of all evil" is a popular saying, but it's not entirely accurate. It is often attributed to the Bible, but it is a misquote of 1 Timothy 6:10 which states, "For the love of money is a root of all kinds of evil. Some people, eager for money, have wandered from the faith and pierced themselves with many griefs."

Money itself is not evil, it is a neutral tool that can be used for both good and bad purposes. It can provide for basic needs such as food, shelter, and clothing, and can also be used to help others and to support charitable causes.

However, the love of money, or the excessive desire for wealth and material possessions, can lead to negative consequences such as greed, selfishness, and a lack of empathy for others. It can also lead to unethical behavior, such as taking advantage of others or engaging in illegal activities to acquire wealth.

It's important to have a healthy relationship with money, to understand the role it plays in our lives and to use it in a responsible and ethical way. It's important to prioritize our values and to use money in a way that aligns with our personal and moral principles.

In conclusion, money itself is not evil, but the love of it can lead to negative consequences. It's important to have a healthy relationship with money and to use it in a responsible and ethical way.

Empowering ways to share your success

Share your story and experiences with others through speaking engagements, mentoring, or writing articles or books.

Use social media to showcase your accomplishments and share valuable information or tips with your followers.

Collaborate with others in your industry or field to create joint ventures, projects or products.

Share your success by giving back to your community through volunteering, mentoring, or philanthropy.

Share your knowledge and skills by teaching a class or workshop.

Network and build relationships with other successful individuals and organizations to expand your reach and impact.

Celebrate and recognize the accomplishments of your team, colleagues, and partners to show that success is a collective effort.

How is success a collective effort

Success is often a collective effort because it often involves the contributions and efforts of multiple individuals and groups working together towards a common goal. For example, in a business setting, success may be achieved through the efforts of employees, managers, and executives working together to achieve a company's goals. In a sports team, success may be achieved through the coordinated efforts of players, coaches, and support staff. Similarly, in a community or non-profit setting, success may be achieved through the efforts of volunteers, donors, and community leaders working together to make a positive impact.

Additionally, many successful individuals often rely on the support and guidance of mentors, coaches, and other experienced individuals to help them achieve their goals. Furthermore, access to resources, funding, networks, and other key elements also play a role in success. Therefore, success is not only the result of individual efforts, but also the result of the collective efforts of many people working together towards a common goal.

Most effective ways of bringing people together to ensure the success of a project

Clearly communicate the goals and objectives of the project: Make sure everyone understands the purpose and importance of the project and how their efforts will contribute to its success.

Build a strong team: Assemble a team of people with different skills and perspectives to ensure a well-rounded approach. Encourage collaboration and teamwork among team members.

Establish a clear plan and timeline: Outline the steps and milestones needed to complete the project, and assign specific tasks and responsibilities to team members.

Encourage open communication: Foster an environment where team members feel comfortable sharing their ideas and concerns. Regular meetings and check-ins can help keep everyone on the same page.

Reward and recognize contributions: Recognize and appreciate the efforts of team members, and celebrate milestones and successes along the way.

Assign a strong leader: Appoint a leader who can effectively manage the team, delegate tasks, and make important decisions.

Encourage creativity and innovation: Encourage team members to think outside the box and come up with new and creative solutions to challenges.

Embrace diversity and inclusivity: Encourage diversity in the team and ensure that everyone feels heard and valued.

Be adaptable and flexible: Be open to change and willing to adjust the plan if necessary.

Address conflicts promptly: Address any conflicts or issues that may arise among team members and take steps to resolve them quickly.

By utilizing these methods you can bring people together to work towards a common goal, and increase the chances of success for the project.

How to overcome the barriers to personal success

Set clear and specific goals: Define what you want to achieve and establish a plan for how to reach those goals.

Identify and overcome limiting beliefs: Be aware of any negative thoughts or beliefs that may be holding you back and work to overcome them.

Develop a growth mindset: Embrace challenges and setbacks as opportunities for growth and learning.

Take action and be consistent: Take consistent and purposeful steps towards achieving your goals, and don't give up easily.

Build a support system: Surround yourself with positive and supportive people who can provide guidance and encouragement.

Learn from failure: Don't be afraid to fail, and use failure as a learning opportunity to adjust your approach and try again.

Stay organized and manage your time effectively: Prioritize your tasks and manage your time effectively to make the most of your efforts.

Stay positive and persistent: Keep a positive attitude and stay persistent in your efforts, even when faced with obstacles.

Continuously improve and learn: Seek out opportunities for learning and personal development, and always strive to improve yourself.

Be accountable: Take responsibility for your actions and stay accountable for the progress you make towards achieving your goals.

By working on these points, you can overcome the barriers to personal success and achieve your goals. Remember that progress takes time and effort, and it's okay to make mistakes along the way. Keep in mind that success is not a destination, but a continuous journey of self-improvement and growth.

Build your team

How to become the best manager of any team

Communicate effectively: Clearly communicate goals, expectations, and feedback to team members. Encourage open communication and actively listen to feedback and concerns.

Lead by example: Demonstrate the behavior and work ethic that you expect from your team.

Set clear goals and expectations: Clearly define what success looks like for the team and individual team members, and set measurable goals to track progress.

Empower and trust your team: Give team members autonomy and trust them to make decisions and take ownership of their work.

Develop your team: Invest in the professional development of your team members and provide opportunities for them to learn and grow.

Be adaptable and flexible: Be open to change and willing to adjust your management style and approach to best suit the needs of your team.

Build a positive culture: Foster a positive and inclusive team culture, and actively work to build morale and motivation.

Lead with integrity: Lead with integrity and honesty, and hold yourself accountable for your actions.

Be available and approachable: Be available and approachable to your team, and make sure they know they can come to you with any concerns or questions.

Recognize and reward success: Recognize and reward the efforts and successes of your team members, and celebrate the team's accomplishments.

By focusing on these points, you can become an effective manager and lead a successful team. Remember that being a great manager is not only about achieving your goals, but also developing and motivating your team members to be the best they can be.

Succeed at pitching your business idea

Clearly communicate your value proposition: Clearly and concisely explain how your business will solve a problem or fill a need in the market.

Tell a compelling story: Use storytelling to convey the passion and vision behind your business, and why it matters.

Be prepared and confident: Practice your pitch and be prepared to answer any questions that may arise. Speak with confidence and enthusiasm, and be able to clearly convey the key points of your pitch.

Use visuals and data to support your pitch: Use charts, graphs, and other visual aids to help illustrate key points and make your pitch more engaging. Use data and research to back up your claims and demonstrate the potential for success.

Identify and address potential objections: Anticipate potential objections and be prepared to address them. This will show that you have thought through the potential challenges and have a plan to overcome them.

Tailor your pitch to your audience: Tailor your pitch to the specific needs and interests of your audience. Be aware of their perspective and tailor your pitch accordingly.

Show your team and traction: If you have a team, introduce them, and if possible show traction, like customers, partnerships, or revenue.

Follow up after the pitch: Follow up with your audience after the pitch to continue the conversation and address any additional questions or concerns they may have.

Be ready to negotiate: Be prepared to negotiate and be open to feedback, and be willing to make changes to your pitch if necessary.

Have a next step ready: Have a clear next step in mind for what you want your audience to do after hearing your pitch, whether that's making an investment, joining your team, or providing feedback.

By focusing on these points, you can increase your chances of successfully pitching your business idea and convincing potential investors or partners to get on board with your vision. Remember that a great pitch is not only about the words you say but also the way you say it, your body language and your overall presence.

Empowering Success Sharing Ways

Empowering ways to share your success

Share your story and experiences with others through speaking engagements, mentoring, or writing articles or books.

Use social media to showcase your accomplishments and share valuable information or tips with your followers.

Collaborate with others in your industry or field to create joint ventures, projects or products.

Share your success by giving back to your community through volunteering, mentoring, or philanthropy.

Share your knowledge and skills by teaching a class or workshop.

Network and build relationships with other successful individuals and organizations to expand your reach and impact.

Celebrate and recognize the accomplishments of your team, colleagues, and partners to show that success is a collective effort

Learning from your mistakes is the key to becoming a success in anything

Learning from your mistakes is an important aspect of achieving success in any endeavor. Failure can be a valuable teacher, it can provide valuable insights and information on what works and what doesn't, and help you make adjustments to your approach. It can also help you develop resilience, perseverance, and a growth mindset, which are all important qualities for achieving success.

However, it's not the only key to becoming a success. There are many other factors that contribute to success, such as hard work, determination, strategic planning, and a positive attitude. Additionally, having a clear goal and a plan for how to achieve it, being organized and managing your time effectively, seeking out opportunities for learning and personal development, and surrounding yourself with positive and supportive people are also crucial.

It's also important to note that success is a relative term and it can mean different things to different people. Success can be defined in many ways, such as achieving financial stability, fulfilling personal aspirations, making a positive impact in the community, or even simply being happy and fulfilled.

In summary, learning from mistakes is certainly important, but it's just one piece of the puzzle. A combination of several factors, including learning from mistakes, hard work, positive attitude, and focus on a clear goal, are key to achieving success in any endeavor.

Top 10 quotes about success

"Success is not the key to happiness. Happiness is the key to success. If you love what you are doing, you will be successful." - Albert Schweitzer

"Success is not final, failure is not fatal: It is the courage to continue that counts." - Winston Churchill

"Success is not the result of spontaneous combustion. You must set yourself on fire." - Arnold H. Glasow

"Success is not how high you have climbed, but how you make a positive difference to the world." - Roy T. Bennett

"Success is not the key to happiness. Happiness is the key to success. If you love what you are doing, you will be successful." - Albert Schweitzer

"Success is not the absence of failure; it's the persistence through failure." - Aisha Tyler

"Success is not how much money you make, but the difference you make in people's lives." - Michelle Obama

"Success is not the key to happiness. Happiness is the key to success. If you love what you are doing, you will be successful." - Herman Cain

"Success is not final, failure is not fatal: It is the courage to continue that counts." - Ernest Hemingway

"Success is not the key to happiness. Happiness is the key to success. If you love what you are doing, you will be successful." - H. Jackson Brown Jr.

How to become the best manager of any team

Communicate effectively: Clearly communicate goals, expectations, and feedback to team members. Encourage open communication and actively listen to feedback and concerns.

Lead by example: Demonstrate the behavior and work ethic that you expect from your team.

Set clear goals and expectations: Clearly define what success looks like for the team and individual team members, and set measurable goals to track progress.

Empower and trust your team: Give team members autonomy and trust them to make decisions and take ownership of their work.

Develop your team: Invest in the professional development of your team members and provide opportunities for them to learn and grow.

Be adaptable and flexible: Be open to change and willing to adjust your management style and approach to best suit the needs of your team.

Build a positive culture: Foster a positive and inclusive team culture, and actively work to build morale and motivation.

Lead with integrity: Lead with integrity and honesty, and hold yourself accountable for your actions.

Be available and approachable: Be available and approachable to your team, and make sure they know they can come to you with any concerns or questions.

Recognize and reward success: Recognize and reward the efforts and successes of your team members, and celebrate the team's accomplishments.

By focusing on these points, you can become an effective manager and lead a successful team. Remember that being a great manager is not only about achieving your goals, but also developing and motivating your team members to be the best they can be.

Building on success to create a legacy

Continuously strive for excellence: Build on your successes by setting new goals and continuously striving for excellence in your work.

Innovate and adapt: Stay ahead of the curve by being open to new ideas and continuously innovating and adapting to changes in your industry.

Invest in your team: Invest in the development and growth of your team members and create opportunities for them to succeed.

Give back to the community: Give back to the community by supporting charitable causes and organizations that align with your values.

Create a strong brand: Develop a strong and recognizable brand that reflects the values and mission of your business.

Embrace transparency and integrity: Embrace transparency and integrity in your business practices and build trust with your stakeholders.

Foster a positive culture: Foster a positive and inclusive culture within your organization that encourages creativity, innovation, and teamwork.

Leave a lasting impact: Seek out opportunities to make a lasting impact in your industry and community.

Document and share your story: Document and share your story through writing, speaking engagements, and other means to inspire others and leave a legacy.

Plan for the future: Plan for the long-term success of your business by creating a strategic plan that considers potential challenges and opportunities.

By focusing on these points, you can build on your successes to create a lasting legacy in your industry and community. Remember that creating a legacy is not only about achieving success, but also about making a positive impact and leaving a lasting legacy for future generations.

Becoming a success in a recession

Stay agile and adaptable: Be prepared to adapt to changes in the market and adjust your business strategy as needed.

Focus on cost-cutting: Look for ways to cut costs and increase efficiency, such as streamlining processes, renegotiating vendor contracts, and reducing overhead expenses.

Diversify your revenue streams: Look for new revenue streams and diversify your income to reduce dependence on any one source.

Invest in marketing and sales: Invest in marketing and sales efforts to attract new customers and maintain relationships with existing ones.

Prioritize customer service: Prioritize providing excellent customer service to retain current customers and attract new ones.

Embrace technology: Embrace technology to automate processes, improve efficiency, and reduce costs.

Utilize government resources: Research and take advantage of government resources such as grants, loans, and tax incentives that are available during a recession.

Network and collaborate: Network with other businesses and industry leaders to share resources and collaborate on projects.

Look for opportunities: Stay informed about market trends and look for opportunities that may arise during a recession.

Stay positive and persistent: Stay positive and persistent in the face of challenges, and remember that recessions are often followed by periods of growth and opportunity.

By focusing on these points, you can increase your chances of success during a recession. Remember that recessions can be difficult times for businesses, but with the right strategy, mindset, and effort, it is possible to not only survive but also thrive during these times.

Healthy ways to enjoy success

Practice gratitude: Take time to appreciate and give thanks for your accomplishments and the people who have helped you along the way.

How to practice gratitude

Start a gratitude journal: Write down things that you're grateful for each day, no matter how small they may seem.

Share your gratitude with others: Tell someone you appreciate them or write a thank-you note.

Reflect on past blessings: Think about all the good things that have happened in your life and how they've shaped you.

Practice mindfulness: Take a moment to focus on the present and appreciate what's around you.

Give back: Helping others can bring a sense of purpose and gratitude.

Incorporate it in your daily routine: Make it a habit to express gratitude before going to sleep or after waking up.

Keep a gratitude jar: Place notes of things you're grateful for in a jar and read them when you need a boost.

Live in the moment: Appreciate the small things in life and enjoy the journey, not just the destination.

Remember, gratitude is a practice, not a destination. It takes time and effort to make it a habit, but the benefits are worth it in the long run.

Set new goals: Set new goals to strive for and continue to challenge yourself.

How to set new goals

Start by identifying your current situation and what you want to achieve.

Set specific, measurable, attainable, relevant, and time-bound (SMART) goals.

Break down larger goals into smaller, more manageable steps.

Create a plan of action for achieving each step.

Set a deadline for achieving each goal.

Review and adjust your goals as needed.

Take action and work towards achieving your goals every day.

Celebrate and share your success: Share your success with others, and celebrate your accomplishments with friends, family, and colleagues.

Prioritize self-care: Make sure to take care of yourself physically, emotionally, and mentally.

Tips on self care on a journey to success

Prioritize self-care: Make sure to set aside time each day to take care of yourself, whether it's exercise, meditation, or just taking a relaxing bath.

Get enough sleep: Make sure to get at least 7-8 hours of sleep each night to help your mind and body function at their best.

Eat well: Eating a healthy and balanced diet can help you feel energized and focused.

Exercise regularly: Regular physical activity can help reduce stress, improve mental health, and boost energy levels.

Connect with others: Surround yourself with supportive people and make time for social connections.

Learn to manage stress: Practice stress-reduction techniques such as deep breathing, yoga, or mindfulness.

Take time for yourself: Make sure to set aside time for hobbies and activities that bring you joy and relaxation.

Prioritize mental health: Don't hesitate to seek professional help if you're struggling with mental health issues, such as anxiety or depression.

Be kind to yourself: Be gentle and compassionate towards yourself. Recognize that success is a journey and setbacks are normal part of it.

Remember to celebrate small wins: Recognize and celebrate your achievements, no matter how small they may be. This will keep you motivated and help you maintain a positive attitude.

Give back to others: Use your success to make a positive impact on others by volunteering, mentoring, or supporting charitable causes.

Be humble: Stay humble and grounded, and avoid becoming arrogant or complacent.

Learn from failures: Learn from any failures or setbacks and use them to grow and improve.

Keep a positive perspective: Stay positive and optimistic, and avoid getting caught up in negative thoughts or emotions.

Stay true to your values: Stay true to your values and principles, and don't compromise them for the sake of success.

Dangers of compromising your values when seeking success

Compromising your values in the pursuit of success can have several negative consequences:

Loss of integrity: When you compromise your values, you may lose trust in yourself and others may lose trust in you. This can damage your reputation and make it difficult to achieve your goals in the long run.

Inner turmoil: Compromising your values can lead to feelings of guilt, shame, and inner turmoil. This can negatively impact your mental and emotional well-being.

Loss of motivation: When you don't align your actions with your values, you may lose motivation and passion for what you're doing. This can make it harder to achieve success.

Missed opportunities: Holding true to your values can open up new opportunities and possibilities that align with your values and purpose.

Damaged relationships: Compromising your values can also lead to conflicts and damaged relationships with family, friends, and colleagues.

Ethical issues: Compromising your values can also lead to ethical issues such as exploitation, fraud, and discrimination.

Enjoy the journey: Remember that success is a journey, not a destination. Take time to enjoy the process, and appreciate the small wins along the way.

By focusing on these points, you can enjoy your success in a healthy and balanced way. Remember that success is not only about achieving your goals, but also about how you feel about yourself and the impact you have on others.

Avoiding Business Sharks

How to a be shark not shark bait in business

To avoid being "shark bait" in business, you should focus on building a strong foundation for your company, including a solid business plan, a clear understanding of your target market, and a unique value proposition. Additionally, it's important to stay current with industry trends and developments, and to constantly be looking for new ways to innovate and stay ahead of the competition.

Building relationships with other businesses and industry leaders can also be beneficial, as they can provide valuable connections and resources. Finally, be prepared for challenges and setbacks, and don't be afraid to take calculated risks in order to grow your business.

When you become a success what comes next

When you achieve success, there are several things that may come next. Some possible outcomes include:

Set new goals: Success often leads to the desire to set new and bigger goals, and to continue growing and improving.

Help others: Many successful people use their experience, resources, and influence to help others achieve their goals and improve their lives.

Maintaining success: Success is often a continuous process and requires effort to maintain. Successful people often have to continue to work hard to stay on top and defend their position.

Enjoy the fruits of your labor: After working hard to achieve success, many people enjoy the rewards and benefits that come with it, such as financial security, personal satisfaction, and a sense of accomplishment.

Reflect and Learn: Successful people often take time to reflect on their journey and learn from their experiences, both positive and negative, to improve for the future.

It's worth noting that success is a personal concept and it can mean different things to different people. Therefore, what comes next after achieving success, can vary greatly depending on one's personal goals, values, and vision.

2) Think of creating a course to help people achieve success in their life

Here is an outline for a course that could help people achieve success in their life:

Module 1: Setting and Achieving Goals

Defining success and setting clear and measurable goals

Creating a plan of action to achieve goals

Identifying and overcoming obstacles that may prevent success

Module 1: Defining and Setting Goals

Understanding the importance of goal-setting in achieving success

Identifying personal values and aligning goals with them

Setting SMART (Specific, Measurable, Achievable, Relevant, and Time-bound) goals

Creating a plan of action to achieve goals

Module 2: Overcoming Obstacles

Identifying and overcoming common obstacles that may prevent success

Developing problem-solving and critical-thinking skills

Building resilience and learning from failures

Module 3: Time Management and Prioritization

Identifying and prioritizing important tasks

Using tools and techniques to increase efficiency and productivity

Staying organized and avoiding procrastination

Module 4: Mindset and Motivation

Understanding the role of mindset in achieving goals

Developing a growth mindset and learning from failures

Identifying and utilizing personal motivators

Module 5: Accountability and Tracking Progress

Holding oneself accountable for progress and results

Tracking progress and measuring success

Making adjustments and modifying goals as needed

Module 6: Celebrating Success

Recognizing and celebrating small wins along the way

Reflecting on the journey and lessons learned

Setting new goals and continuing the process

Module 2: Time Management and Productivity

Identifying and prioritizing important tasks

Using tools and techniques to increase efficiency and productivity

Managing distractions and staying focused

Module 2: Understanding Time Management

Defining time management and its importance in achieving success

Identifying common time-wasters and distractions

Assessing personal time management skills and setting goals for improvement

Module 2: Prioritization and Goal Setting

Identifying and prioritizing important tasks

Setting SMART (Specific, Measurable, Achievable, Relevant, and Time-bound) goals

Developing a plan of action to achieve goals

Module 3: Productivity Techniques

Learning and implementing productivity techniques such as the Pomodoro technique, time blocking and the Eisenhower matrix

Using tools and apps to increase efficiency and productivity

Staying organized and avoiding procrastination

Module 4: Mindset and Motivation

Understanding the role of mindset in productivity

Developing a growth mindset and learning from failures

Identifying and utilizing personal motivators

Module 5: Managing Distractions

Identifying and managing common distractions such as social media, email, and interruptions

Building focus and concentration

Managing external and internal distractions

Module 6: Flexibility and Adaptability

Understanding the importance of being adaptable and open to change

Developing strategies for dealing with change and uncertainty

Embracing new opportunities and taking calculated risks

Module 3: Mindset and Motivation

Understanding the role of mindset in achieving success

Developing a growth mindset and learning from failures

Identifying and utilizing personal motivators

Module 4: Personal Development

Building self-awareness and understanding personal strengths and weaknesses

Improving communication and interpersonal skills

Developing a positive self-image and self-confidence

Module 1: Understanding Mindset

Defining mindset and its role in achieving success

Identifying the difference between a fixed and growth mindset

Assessing personal mindset and setting goals for improvement

Module 2: Overcoming Limiting Beliefs

Identifying and challenging limiting beliefs

Building self-awareness and understanding personal strengths and weaknesses

Developing a positive self-image and self-confidence

Module 3: Setting and Achieving Goals

Understanding the importance of goal-setting in motivation

Setting SMART (Specific, Measurable, Achievable, Relevant, and Time-bound) goals

Creating a plan of action to achieve goals

Module 4: Motivation Techniques

Identifying personal motivators and utilizing them

Learning and implementing motivation techniques such as visualization, affirmations and creating a vision board

Staying motivated and on track towards achieving goals

Module 5: Building Resilience

Understanding the role of resilience in achieving success

Developing problem-solving and critical-thinking skills

Building resilience and learning from failures

Module 6: Emotional Intelligence

Understanding the importance of emotional intelligence in motivation and success

Building self-awareness, empathy and emotional regulation

Utilizing emotional intelligence to build better relationships

Module 5: Networking and Building Relationships

Building and nurturing a professional and personal network

Mastering the art of networking and making connections

Understanding the importance of relationships in achieving success

Secrets to Networking and Building Relationships

Here is an overview of some "secrets" to networking and building relationships:

Be authentic: Be true to yourself and your intentions when networking. People can sense insincerity, and it's hard to build genuine relationships when you're not being genuine.

Be a good listener: People love to talk about themselves, and when you listen actively and show genuine interest in what they have to say, they will be more likely to remember you and want to build a relationship.

Follow up: After making a new connection, be sure to follow up with them. Send them an email or a LinkedIn message, and try to schedule a call or meeting.

Provide value: Look for ways to help others and provide value to your connections. Whether it's introducing them to someone in your network or sharing valuable information, people are more likely to want to build a relationship with someone who they perceive as helpful.

Be consistent: Building relationships takes time, so be consistent in your efforts. Follow up with your connections regularly and make an effort to stay in touch.

Leverage social media: Social media platforms like LinkedIn, Twitter, and Facebook can be powerful tools for building and maintaining relationships. Connect with people in your industry, share valuable content, and engage in online conversations.

Be patient: Building relationships is a process and it takes time, so be patient. Keep in mind that not all connections will lead to immediate opportunities, but over time, a strong network will open doors for you.

Give before you take: Approach networking and building relationships with the mindset of giving before you take. This means that you should focus on helping others and providing value, rather than always looking for ways to get something out of the relationship.

It's important to remember that networking and building relationships are not just about getting something from the other person, it's about building mutually beneficial connections.

Module 6: Financial Management

Understanding the importance of financial literacy

Creating a budget and managing expenses

Investing for the future and creating a plan for financial security

Successful financial management

Here is an overview of some strategies for successful financial management:

Create a budget: One of the most important steps in financial management is creating a budget. A budget allows you to track your income and expenses, identify areas where you can cut back, and plan for future expenses.

Save for emergencies: Having an emergency fund can help you weather unexpected events such as job loss, medical emergencies or home repairs. Aim for saving at least 3-6 months of living expenses in an emergency fund.

Pay off debt: High-interest debt can be a major obstacle to achieving financial stability. Prioritize paying off high-interest debt such as credit card balances, personal loans, and installment loans.

Invest for the future: Investing in assets such as stocks, bonds, or real estate can help grow your wealth over time. Consider seeking professional advice if you're unsure where to start.

Plan for retirement: Start planning for retirement as early as possible, as it will give you more time to save and invest. Consider opening a retirement account, such as an IRA or 401(k), and start contributing to it as soon as possible.

Be mindful of taxes: Keep track of the taxes you owe and take advantage of tax-saving opportunities. Consult a tax professional if you need help understanding the tax laws and regulations.

Continuously educate yourself: Stay informed about the financial markets, tax laws, and other financial topics. This will help you make informed decisions and avoid costly mistakes.

Review your progress and adjust as needed: Review your budget and financial plan regularly and adjust as needed. Be open to making changes in your spending habits and investment strategy as your goals and circumstances change.

It's important to remember that successful financial management is a continuous process, it requires discipline, patience and consistency. It's also crucial to set realistic financial goals and to review and adjust them as your situation change.

Module 7: Adapting to change

Understanding the importance of being adaptable and open to change

Developing strategies for dealing with change and uncertainty

Embracing new opportunities and taking calculated risks

How to Develop strategies for dealing with change and uncertainty

Here are some strategies for developing strategies for dealing with change and uncertainty:

Embrace change: Recognize that change is a natural part of life and can bring new opportunities. Try to approach change with a positive attitude and an open mind.

Be proactive: Rather than waiting for change to happen to you, take the initiative to create change. Identify areas of your life that you want to improve and develop a plan to make it happen.

Develop a growth mindset: A growth mindset focuses on learning and improvement, rather than on fixed abilities. This mindset can help you adapt to change and uncertainty.

Learn to adapt: Develop the skills and abilities that will help you adapt to new situations. This might include learning a new language, taking a course, or learning new software.

Build a support system: Surround yourself with people who will support and encourage you during times of change and uncertainty. This might include friends, family, or a professional therapist.

Stay organized: Make sure you have a system in place for keeping track of important information and deadlines. This will help you stay on top of things even when things are changing rapidly.

Learn to be comfortable with uncertainty: Accept that there will always be elements of uncertainty in life. Learn to be comfortable with not knowing what the future holds and to trust yourself to handle whatever comes your way.

Take calculated risks: Don't let the fear of change and uncertainty hold you back. Take calculated risks and be open to new opportunities that come your way.

It's important to remember that change and uncertainty are a natural part of life, and developing strategies to deal with them can help you become more resilient and better equipped to handle new challenges.

Get funding for your business idea

There are several ways to obtain funding for your business idea, including:

Angel investors: These are high net-worth individuals who invest their own money in start-ups.

Venture capital: Venture capital firms invest in early-stage companies with high growth potential.

Crowdfunding: Platforms like Kickstarter and Indiegogo allow entrepreneurs to raise money from a large number of people.

Bank loans: Banks and other financial institutions may provide loans to small businesses.

Incubators and accelerators: Incubators and accelerators provide funding, mentorship, and other resources to start-ups.

Government grants: Some government agencies provide grants to small businesses for specific purposes such as research and development.

One thing that will make you successful in life

One thing that can contribute to success in life is having a strong work ethic. This includes being disciplined, persistent, and dedicated to achieving your goals. A strong work ethic can help you stay motivated, overcome challenges, and continually improve your skills and knowledge. Additionally, being reliable, punctual, and having a positive attitude can also be key factors in being successful in life.

It's also important to note that success can be defined in many ways, and it's not solely about achieving wealth or fame. Finding balance in your personal and professional life, maintaining healthy relationships and having a sense of purpose are also aspects that can contribute to a successful life.

Why obtaining success in business is hard

Obtaining success in business can be hard for a variety of reasons. Some common challenges include intense competition, the need to constantly adapt to changing market conditions, and the difficulty of predicting and managing risks.

Additionally, starting and growing a business often requires significant financial investment and can be stressful and time-consuming. Furthermore, there are many factors that can affect the success of a business, such as the quality of the product or service, the effectiveness of marketing and sales strategies, and the ability to manage and lead a team.

Lastly the current economic and political situation can also affect the business.

Here are a few quotes from successful people that may inspire you:

"Success is not the key to happiness. Happiness is the key to success. If you love what you are doing, you will be successful." - Albert Schweitzer

"I have not failed. I've just found 10,000 ways that won't work." - Thomas Edison

"If you look at what you have in life, you'll always have more. If you look at what you don't have in life, you'll never have enough." - Oprah Winfrey

"The biggest adventure you can ever take is to live the life of your dreams." - Oprah Winfrey

"The biggest risk is not taking any risk. In a world that's changing quickly, the only strategy that is guaranteed to fail is not taking risks." - Mark Zuckerberg

"Success is not final, failure is not fatal: it is the courage to continue that counts." - Winston Churchill

"I'm convinced that about half of what separates successful entrepreneurs from the non-successful ones is pure perseverance." - Steve Jobs

"The best way to predict your future is to create it." - Abraham Lincoln

"Success is not the absence of failure; it's the persistence through failure." - Aisha Tyler

"The road to success and the road to failure are almost exactly the same." - Colin R. Davis

Best business ideas for 2023

It is difficult to predict the best business ideas for 2023 as it depends on various factors such as economic conditions, market trends, and consumer preferences. However, here are some general business ideas that could potentially be successful in 2023:

E-commerce: With the rise of online shopping, starting an e-commerce business selling unique or niche products could be a good idea.

Health and wellness: With more people focusing on their health and wellness, starting a business in this industry, such as a gym, a healthy food delivery service or a personal training service could be a good idea.

Sustainable products and services: Interest in sustainable products and services is increasing. Starting a business in this field could be a good idea such as recycling, renewable energy, or organic farming.

Technology: With the increasing use of technology, starting a business in fields such as software development, app development, or digital marketing could be a good idea.

Service Industry: Starting a service-based business such as home cleaning, handyman services, or pet-sitting could be a good idea.

Please note that these are just general ideas, and the potential success of a business depends on many factors such as market research, location, and competition among others.

Artificial intelligence

(AI) can help you become successful in a variety of ways, including:

Automation: AI can automate repetitive tasks, such as data entry and analysis, freeing up time and resources for more important tasks.

Decision-making: AI can help you make better decisions by analyzing large amounts of data and identifying patterns and trends that might not be immediately apparent.

Predictive analytics: AI can predict future outcomes based on past data and trends, which can help you plan for the future and make better decisions.

Personalization: AI can personalize products and services to meet the specific needs of individual customers, which can increase customer satisfaction and loyalty.

Cost savings: AI can help you reduce costs by automating tasks, increasing efficiency, and improving decision-making.

Business Intelligence: AI can help you make data-driven decisions and gain insights to improve your business performance.

Robotics and automation: AI can be used to automate repetitive and dangerous tasks and improve production in many industries.

Cybersecurity: AI can help you detect and prevent cyber attacks by identifying and blocking threats in real-time.

Please note that AI is not a magic solution and it needs to be implemented with a strategic plan and with the right resources to be useful.

Investing in Ai could help your success

Where to invest in Ai

There are several ways to invest in Artificial Intelligence (AI), some of which include:

Stock market: Investing in publicly traded companies that are involved in AI technology such as Google, Microsoft, Amazon, and NVIDIA.

AI-focused funds: Investing in funds that specifically focus on companies involved in AI technology and related fields such as machine learning, computer vision, and natural language processing.

Startups: Investing in early-stage AI startups that have the potential to grow and become successful companies.

Real-Estate: Investing in properties that are located in areas where AI research and development is taking place, like universities and research centers.

AI-related ETFs: Investing in exchange-traded funds (ETFs) that track the performance of AI-related companies and industries.

Direct Investment: Investing in companies or projects that are developing AI technologies, such as robotics, natural language processing, or machine learning.

It's important to note that investing always involves risk and you should conduct thorough research and consult with a financial advisor before making any investment decisions.

How to be successful in love

Being successful in love can be challenging, but there are some things you can do to increase your chances of finding and maintaining a healthy, happy relationship:

Be confident: Believe in yourself and your worth as a person. Confidence can make you more attractive to others and help you to communicate effectively.

Communicate openly and honestly: Share your feelings, thoughts, and concerns with your partner and actively listen to them.

Be respectful: Show respect for your partner's feelings, opinions, and boundaries.

Show appreciation: Express gratitude and appreciation for your partner, and let them know that you value and appreciate them.

Be supportive: Offer emotional and practical support when your partner needs it.

Be flexible: Be open to compromise and change, and be willing to adapt to your partner's needs and wants.

Be self-aware: Understand your own needs, wants and emotions, and work on self-improvement.

Learn to forgive: Learn to forgive your partner and yourself for mistakes, and work on resolving conflicts in a healthy way.

Keep the spark alive: Keep the relationship exciting by trying new things and doing things together.

Seek help: Don't be afraid to seek help from a therapist or counselor if you need it.

Remember that love is a continuous process, it requires effort and patience from both partners, and it is different for everyone.

Blueprint for a successful business

A successful business typically has the following elements:

A clear and compelling business model that outlines how the company will make money.

A well-defined target market and a deep understanding of customer needs and preferences.

Strong and capable leadership, with a clear vision and the ability to execute on that vision.

A solid financial plan, including projections for revenue and expenses and a strategy for securing funding.

A strong and dedicated team, with the skills and experience needed to execute the business plan.

A robust marketing and sales strategy, including a clear value proposition, effective branding, and a well-executed go-to-market plan.

A culture of innovation and continuous improvement, with a focus on staying ahead of the competition and adapting to changing market conditions.

A well-defined set of values and a strong sense of purpose that guides the company's decision-making and actions.

A strong online presence and social media strategy is important for most businesses today.

A solid understanding of legal and compliance requirements,

and a plan for ensuring compliance

Now go and become a success in your own life and spread the Joy

www.ingramcontent.com/pod-product-compliance
Lightning Source LLC
Chambersburg PA
CBHW070310220526
45465CB00004B/1830